Squirrel

Susan Gates

Illustrated by
Tony Kerins

OXFORD
UNIVERSITY PRESS

OXFORD
UNIVERSITY PRESS

Great Clarendon Street, Oxford OX2 6DP

Oxford University Press is a department of the University of Oxford.
It furthers the University's objective of excellence in research, scholarship,
and education by publishing worldwide in

Oxford New York

Auckland Bangkok Buenos Aires Cape Town Chennai
Dar es Salaam Delhi Hong Kong Istanbul Karachi Kolkata
Kuala Lumpur Madrid Melbourne Mexico City Mumbai
Nairobi São Paulo Shanghai Taipei Tokyo Toronto

Oxford is a registered trade mark of Oxford University Press
in the UK and in certain other countries

Database right Oxford University Press (maker)

First published 2003

British Library Cataloguing in Publication Data

Data available

ISBN 0 19 919584 6

3 5 7 9 10 8 6 4 2

Mixed Pack (1 of 6 different titles): ISBN 0 19 919586 2
Class Pack (6 copies of 6 titles): ISBN 0 19 919585 4

Printed in Hong Kong

Contents

Chapter **1**

Squirrel Comes to Stay

Dad undid his coat.

"Alex! Look what I've got," he said. There was a squirrel hanging on to his jumper! He was tiny, just a baby. He was fast asleep.

"Awww," I said. "He's really cute. Where did you get him, Dad?"

"It's a sad story," said Dad. "Listen …"

Dad was walking in the forest. He met some men cutting down trees. One of the men said, "Want a squirrel?"

"Pardon?" said Dad.

"A baby squirrel," said the man. "The tree we cut down had a squirrel's nest in it. His mother was killed. He's too little to look after himself."

"Give him to me," said Dad. "I'll look after him."

So that's how Dad came home with Squirrel.

Dad was at work all day. Mum was
busy. So I had to look after Squirrel.

At first it wasn't hard. He slept all day,
like a newborn baby. He even went to
sleep in my pocket!

"Hey," I told Dad. "Squirrel thinks I'm
a tree. And my pocket is his nest."

I went outside with Squirrel in
my pocket. I walked up and down
the street.

"Alex!" said my friend. "There's a tail
hanging out of your pocket!"

"It's only Squirrel," I said. "He thinks
I'm a tree."

Sometimes, Squirrel would wake up
and eat a nut. Then he'd go to sleep
again. At night, he slept in our old
hamster cage.

I told Dad, "Looking after baby
squirrels is easy. They're no trouble
at all."

Chapter 2

Squirrel Becomes a Pain in the Neck

Then, Squirrel got bigger. He didn't sleep so much. And he wouldn't stay in my pocket.

"Mum!" I shouted. "Come quick!"

Squirrel had run down my leg! Then he'd run back up – INSIDE my trousers!

"Help!" I shouted. "He's run up my trousers!"

I could feel his
sharp little claws.
"He's under
my T-shirt now!"

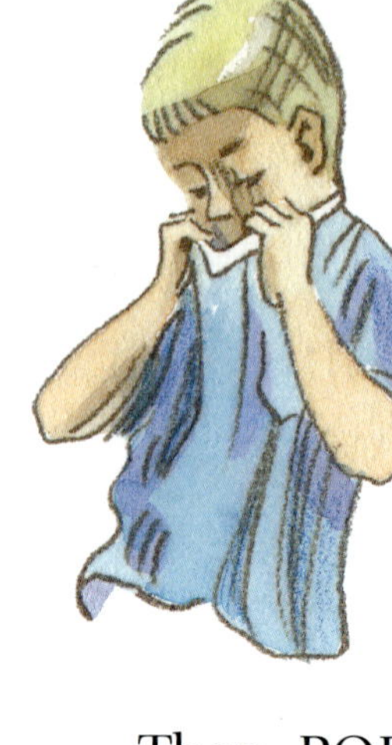

Then, POP!
Squirrel came out
by my neck. He sat
on my shoulder.
Then he climbed
a bit higher.

"He's on top of
my head!"
"I can see that,"
said Mum. "He
thinks you're a tree."

Squirrel got even braver. He stopped
climbing on me. And he started
to climb the curtains.

"Mum!" I shouted.

"Look at Squirrel!"

Mum came rushing in.

Squirrel was sitting on the curtain rail.
He was eating a nut. There were bits of
nut all over the carpet.

Mum said, "Look at the mess your
squirrel's making!"

"*My* squirrel!" I said. "Dad brought
him home!

I tried to stop Squirrel. I really did. But I couldn't. He was wrecking our house. No one thought he was cute any more.

"Squirrel will have to go," said Dad.

"Oh, but Dad," I begged. He's too little to look after himself."

Chapter 3

Squirrel Does His Worst Thing Yet

Then, Squirrel did something really dangerous.

Mum's friend came to visit with her new baby.

Mum said, "Shut Squirrel up in his cage."

I meant to do it. I really did. But there was something good on telly. So I forgot.

Mum's friend came into the room. She was carrying her new baby. He had a pink, bald head.

Suddenly, Squirrel jumped from the curtains. He flew through the air, with his claws out. He was looking for somewhere to land.

"Watch out!" cried Mum. "Mind the baby's head!"

Just in time, the baby's mum turned round. Squirrel missed the baby's head. But he landed on her back.

"Get it off me!" she shouted.

I said, "He can't help it. He thinks you're a tree."

But no one was listening.

"I'm sorry, Alex," said Dad, after they'd gone. "That baby could have been badly hurt. Squirrel will have to go!"

Chapter **4**

Squirrel Gets a Second Chance

So we took Squirrel back to the forest. We left him under a tree with a pile of nuts. He looked so small and sad, sitting there.

I told Dad, "He doesn't know about forests. He's never even climbed a tree!"

"He'll be all right," said Dad. "Walk away and don't look back."

All night, I worried about Squirrel. It
was stormy outside. I thought, "What if
he's scared?"

Next morning, I begged Dad, "Can we go to the forest? Please! Just to see if he's all right? Please!"

Dad said, "All right. But you'll never find him. He's probably miles away by now."

But Squirrel was still there! He was
just where we'd left him.

"See, Dad!" I said. "I told you he was
too little to look after himself."

There were some ladies sitting at a
picnic table. I walked past them.

"Squirrel!" I said.

He was really pleased to see me.
He ran straight up my trousers!
   The ladies' mouths hung open.
   Their eyes almost popped out
of their heads.

"Did you see what that squirrel
just did?"

I tried to look cool. I tried to look
as if squirrels ran up my trouserlegs
all the time.

"He thinks I'm a tree," I told them.
I walked off, with Squirrel sitting on
my head.

Chapter 5

Squirrel is Back Where He Belongs

Two weeks later, Mum said, "I'm sick of finding nuts down the sofa."

Dad said, "He's chewed up my computer disks again."

And I knew we couldn't put it off any longer. This time, Squirrel really had to go.

We took him to the forest again.
We put him under a tree. I said to Dad,
"He won't climb it!"

But then, with a flick of his tail,
he was gone.

"He's there. No, there!" I said.

He shot right to the top of the tree.
Then he was leaping from tree-top to
tree-top. It was as if he'd lived in the
forest all his life.

Suddenly, I couldn't see him any more.
"He's gone," I said, sadly.

We walked back to the car. Dad said,
"He belongs in the forest. You can't keep
squirrels as pets."

I said, "I know that."

But that doesn't stop me thinking about Squirrel. I often wonder where he is. And I hope he's safe and well.

If you're ever walking in a forest, and a squirrel runs up your trousers, you'll tell me, won't you?

About the author

This story is true. Everything in it really happened. When my son Alex was six his dad did bring back a baby squirrel. It started off by being cute and ended up wrecking our house. Take my advice. Never, ever, try to keep a squirrel as a pet. Unless you want chewed chair legs and peanuts in your piano!